Old WEST CALDER

by
William F. Hendrie

To Olive, who enjoyed growing up in West Calder.

West Calder Station opened in 1869 and this photograph was taken 100 years later.

ISBN 1 84033 310 3

**The publishers regret that they cannot supply
copies of any pictures featured in this book.**

ACKNOWLEDGEMENTS

The author and publishers would like to thank West Lothian Local History Librarian Sybil Cavanagh; William Cochrane; Duncan Collin; Allen Douglas; Robert Grieves (who provided the picture on the inside front cover); Ian Hossack (who provided the pictures on pages 4, 7, 17, 20, 21, 26 and the back cover); Todd MacDonald; David and Margaret Rennie; and Elizabeth Wilson for their help with the preparation of this book.

Murieston Castle, which may have dated to as early as the twelfth century, stood on the banks of the Murieston Burn. Just as Livingston derived its name from the village or 'toun' of servants' homes which grew up around Leving's Castle, it is thought that Murieston took its name from the toun of servants' cottages which grew up around Murray's Castle, situated some distance to the south of 'Leving's Toun' and now the site of one of the largest private housing developments in the area. The Murray family also later occupied Livingston Peel, and Murrayfield Primary School in neighbouring Blackburn is named after them, with the school badge bearing a sprig of yellow broom which is the Murray clan flower. This postcard view shows Murieston Castle from the north-west. The corbelled turret appears to have been reached by an entrance at first floor level, and along with the narrow windows was probably originally a defensive feature. In the first *Statistical Account of Scotland*, published at the end of the eighteenth century, Murieston Castle is described as 'an uninhabited fortified peel tower'. Most of its stones had been looted by the time the *New Statistical Account* was published in 1843, possibly to build new farm cottages which were erected in the area during Victorian times. The castle was superseded by the much more comfortable and fashionable Murieston House. According to the *New Statistical Account* this fine two-storey Georgian-style country house, with its pillared porticoed entrance set centrally between the four windows on the ground floor and surmounted by a fanlight, was the family home of Mr James M. Hog. The same volume also states that Mr Hog's neighbours at Wester Murieston were the Keir family.

INTRODUCTION

As its name indicates, West Calder is the most westerly of the three Calders, a group of small towns situated to the south of Livingston New Town. The name Calder is believed to derive from two Celtic words which combine to mean the 'well watered woods'. Indeed, until the latter half of the nineteenth century West Calder was a quiet, rural place. However, the development of shale mining at that time saw it become the centre of the Scottish oil bonanza, along with the neighbouring villages of Addiewell, Bellsquarry and Polbeth.

At a much earlier period in its history, the area now occupied by the three Calders was divided between two large estates: Calder Clere (where East Calder is now situated) and Calder Comitis, where Mid and West Calder are sited. King Malcolm IV granted the former to Randulph de Clere in 1160, while the latter belonged to the Earl or Thane of Fife.

Until 1643 the population of West Calder was served by the Kirk of Calder in neighbouring Mid Calder, but that year the Presbytery of Linlithgow decided that the population had grown to the point where West Calder should be established as a separate parish, and as a result its Auld Kirk was erected. The remains of this historic building still stand as a picturesque, ivy-covered ruin a short distance to the south of the town's Main Street. When still in use as a place of worship, the church was described as 'a plain barn of a place with no pretensions to arched glories' (*Statistical Account of Scotland*). Originally it had only one entrance and when first recognised by the presbytery in 1645 (two years after the creation of the parish), it did not possess any fitted pews. It was typical of Scottish post-Reformation churches with an equally plain exterior, its only adornment being the small belfry, which, although now sadly without its bell, still looks down over the ruins and the surrounding graveyard.

The Auld Kirk served the inhabitants of West Calder until the middle of Queen Victoria's reign when increases in population and the comparative wealth pumped into the local economy by the rise of the Scottish oil industry led to the building of larger, better-lit, more commodious and comfortable churches. Place names such as Kirk Gate and The Glebe (the old Scottish term for the lands that formed part of a minister's benefice, and from which income could be generated by leasing to third parties) are reminders of the church's historic role in West Calder.

The peacefulness of the village was shattered in 1650 when, following the execution the previous year of King Charles I in London, Oliver Cromwell's Republican army encamped in the town. It was on its way north to attempt to deter support in Scotland for the restoration of the monarchy, which it ultimately failed to do as King Charles II was crowned at Scone later that year (although he spent the following decade in exile during the country's brief period of republicanism). After the restoration of the monarchy in 1660 Charles was finally returned to the throne, losing popularity in Scotland because of his enforcement of worship according to his Episcopal beliefs. This resulted in a great deal of support for the Covenanters, those Scots who signed the National Covenant demanding freedom to worship in their own fashion. West Calder's minister became so involved in this religious dispute that he was arrested by the government's redcoat dragoons for his allegedly subversive preaching. The soldiers forced the minister to walk to Edinburgh where he was imprisoned in the old Tolbooth jail on the Royal Mile (where the People's Story museum is now situated). Despite this dramatic event, support for the Covenanters remained strong and many of the minister's congregation showed their solidarity by quitting the Auld Kirk to hold conventicles (open-air acts of worship) in the surrounding hills. They always had to be on guard for approaching soldiers, and at any sign of imminent danger lookouts would alert those attending the service to scatter and hide, sometimes by imitating the cry of the curlew. To help avoid detection the communion vessels were designed so that the bowl, stem and base all came apart so they could be more easily concealed below the worshippers' clothes.

General Tam Dalyell of the House of the Binns near Linlithgow was given responsibility by Charles II for suppressing the Covenanters, and with this aim based his soldiers at West Calder in November 1666. Despite his efforts, which earned him the nickname of 'Bluidy Tam', the Covenanters continued to resist for many more years.

Despite these upheavals, West Calder generally remained a peaceful country parish during the eighteenth and early nineteenth centuries. From the mid-1700s a movement retrospectively called the Agrarian Revolution took place in Scotland in which more modern and efficient farming practices were introduced, leading to higher and more dependable yields from crops. Lime produced locally and used as a fertiliser helped increase production.

A century later the impact of the Industrial Revolution brought far greater prosperity to West Calder when the increased demand for oil led to the development of the Scottish shale oil industry. Such was the extent of this that for a time Scotland led the world in the manufacture of mineral oil products. The pioneer of the process used to extract oil, first from a carboniferous mineral known as Torbanite and subsequently from the much more readily available shale (which lay in abundance beneath the fields around West Calder), was James 'Paraffin' Young, who gained his nickname as a result of his most profitable product.

Young proved as astute a businessman as he was a scientist, and to safeguard his process made certain it was patented not only in Britain but also in the United States. He was equally determined to keep a close personal eye on the development of his refineries and the shale mines which supplied them with their raw material, and bought Limefield, a stylish Georgian-style country house at Polbeth on the eastern outskirts of West Calder. He moved his wife and young family into Limefield, from where he could supervise his industrial empire. James Young also welcomed his former classmate David Livingstone to Limefield, alongside whom he had taken night classes at the Andersonian Institute in Glasgow (to which Strathclyde University owes it origins).

Young's profits from Scottish oil paid for much of Livingstone's explorations and missionary work in Africa, and while staying on furlough at Limefield he performed the official ceremony to mark the beginning of the construction of the nearby Addiewell oil works. Today the sprawling works, with its glowing retorts and forest of tall chimneys, has long since disappeared, but many of the vast bings of spent shale left behind by the process still remain as landmarks (the word bing is derived from the Gaelic *bein* meaning a mountain, as in Ben Nevis and Ben Lomond). West Calder's famous group of bings, known as the Five Sisters, has now been given a category 'A' listing. The group also features as part of West Lothian's armorial bearings, the first time that such a man-made landmark has appeared on a heraldic badge. Special permission from the Lord Lyon, King of Arms, was sought by former councillor and depute provost of West Lothian, Allister Mackie, working in association with the author of this book, to get the bings featured as part of the bearings.

Shale mining, from whose by-products the Five Sisters arose, was always reckoned much safer than coal mining, partly because the deposits were closer to the surface and could be reached by sloping mines rather than deep pits, and partly because the workings were generally free from the presence of methane, or coal damp. Unfortunately, West Calder's Burngrange shale mine proved the exception to this rule and on 10 January 1947 the worst disaster in the history of the Scottish oil industry took place there. Fourteen local shale miners died, suffocated where they worked by carbon monoxide gas followed by a fire. They are still all remembered in West Calder, where to mark the 40th anniversary of their deaths a plaque bearing their names was unveiled in the Main Street.

Although there are still reserves of shale, the Scottish oil industry ceased in 1962, unable to compete with cheaper imported fuel from the Persian Gulf and other foreign sources and made uneconomic by the removal of a preferential tax rate for the home product. The loss of jobs led to a difficult period for West Calder and the surrounding shale oil towns, but now prosperity has returned to the area which is popular with commuters, many of whom work in Edinburgh, Glasgow or Livingston. The town and its neighbours have excellent transport links via the M8 motorway to the cities, whilst West Calder – alone out of the three Calders – has a railway station on the Glasgow Central to Edinburgh Waverley line.

This cast-iron bandstand formerly stood in front of West Calder's library. West Calder Band, founded in 1866, often gave concerts on Sunday afternoons and summer evenings, and such was the enthusiasm for brass band music in the town that bands from neighbouring burghs were also frequently invited to present programmes. The band celebrated its centenary in 1966 and in 1979 acquired new premises in Stewart Street. In the early 1920s this prominent site at the junction of East End, Limefield Road and Harburn Road was selected for the erection of West Calder's war memorial, which was situated adjacent to the bandstand. It initially displayed the names of the men of the town who had given their lives during the First World War, but details of those who fell in the Second World War were later added to the plaques at the foot of the plinth. The war memorial still remains in situ but the bandstand has been removed.

Taken from the top of West Calder's famous former landmark, the Thistle Tower, this picture gives an elevated view of the town on a sunny summer's day at the start of the 1900s as a procession makes its way along Main Street. The original postcard was published by R. Wells Brown, proprietor of the local chemist's (see page 22). This parade may have been organised as part of the Combined Sunday School Outing, a much looked forward to highlight of West Calder summer holidays long before local families were able to afford to fly away on overseas package trips.

Two of West Calder's most familiar buildings, the red sandstone public library and Limefield United Free Church, feature in this view of the east end of the town. The founders of Limefield Free Church (it was only later that it became a United Free Church) believed passionately in the right of members of the congregation – rather than the local landed gentry – to choose their ministers, and were among those who broke away from the Church of Scotland in 1843 in a mass exodus known as the Disruption. The United Free Church reunited with the main body of the Church of Scotland in 1929, but some congregations, including Limefield, chose not to join the Union and retained their independence.

LIBRARY. WEST-CALDER.

Schoolboys with their dog linger beside the railings outside West Calder's ornate library. This opened in 1904, two years after the death of Britain's longest reigning monarch, and has a distinctly art nouveau appearance. The interior features a tiled entrance stairway with stained glass windows, whilst outside the red sandstone lintels are engraved with the words 'History', 'Poetry' and 'Science', reflecting the range of volumes on the library's shelves and in its reference section. The library is operated by West Lothian Council from its headquarters at Blackburn, where local records are available for study. This postcard was sent in October 1904 but the photograph itself may well date from around the time of the library's completion, as two workmen are visible in the picture, one standing precariously on a window sill.

WEST CALDER STATION.

West Calder Station is on the Glasgow to Edinburgh line formerly owned by the Caledonian Railway. At Edinburgh the terminus was originally Princes Street Station, where the Caledonian Hotel still stands, but trains now terminate at Waverley. The line also provides direct connections with Livingston South, Kirknewton and Haymarket to the east, and Addiewell, Breich, Fauldhouse, Shotts, Bellshill, Uddingston and Cambuslang to the west. Services are well-used by West Calder commuters travelling to work in these places and in particular Edinburgh and Glasgow. In addition to regular through and stopping trains on this 46¼ mile southerly route between Glasgow and Edinburgh, a special service was formerly operated each Saturday evening to take West Calder people for a night out in the capital. It was known as the 'ninepenny rattler' because of the reduced return fare and the old rolling stock used. The return service departed from Princes Street Station at 11 p.m. and was often so crowded and rowdy that two uniformed police constables would be on duty to await its arrival at West Calder, where those seen to be drunk were arrested, spending time in the cells at the town's police station before appearing before the bailie, as the magistrate was known, on Monday morning.

THE STATION, WEST CALDER. W.C.12.

The passenger footbridge dominates this view of West Calder Station, with one of the area's many shale bings looming in the background. In addition to the ninepenny rattler, special trains were frequently operated from West Calder Station on days when the local junior football team played away matches so that hundreds of fans could attend these fixtures. The station was such a busy place that it had a staff of over a dozen employees, including the stationmaster who was provided with a house on the site, two booking clerks in the ticket office, two passenger porters, two goods porters and several signalmen. Three coal merchants had their depots in the station yard and much of the coal which arrived by rail was then transported by horse-drawn carts to the town's gasworks. These were founded in 1871 with capital of £2,000 raised in £1 shares. The stationmaster's house, seen on the left, was later converted into a restaurant.

Main Street seen at a time when what little traffic that used it was entirely horse-drawn. The attractive curved forestair on the right led up to what later became the snooker hall owned by Eddie Boyd. Kirkgate leads off to the left at this point, providing access to the Auld Kirk and manse. In 1643 the Presbytery of Linlithgow separated Mid Calder and West Calder into two parishes. Between then and 1645 West Calder's first known place of worship was constructed. The church was abandoned and became a ruin in the latter quarter of the nineteenth century following the shale oil boom and the resultant boost to the local economy which allowed larger and more comfortable churches to be built to serve the growing congregations in the town.

West Calder Co-operative Society was founded in 1874 with capital of £4,588 raised from £1 shares owned by its members. This building, which occupied a prominent site on the south side of Main Street, was its impressive central premises. Today the clock is the only surviving remnant of what was once the society's headquarters, and its re-erection as a decorative feature on the south side of Main Street brings back memories of when the co-op was at its peak. It bears the inscription 'We Strive and We Rise' above its face, a suitable reminder of the success which the co-operative movement enjoyed in the Calders area for a century.

Main Street, West Calder.

West Calder Co-op operated busy branches in neighbouring towns and villages, and also owned the impressive three-storey building seen beyond the premises of the Central Inn on the left of this view. It is now occupied by several privately owned shops. Members had their own co-op numbers which were quoted each time they bought checks – small round tokens with different colours denoting different values – which were used to make payments in the shops. This meant that customers' purchases could all be credited to their numbers, thus ensuring that the profits were fairly shared out when the time came for the quarterly dividend to be paid.

One of the more unusual items sold by West Calder Co-op was gunpowder, used by shot-firers to bring down shale in nearby mines and supplied by the co-op in thick blue paper bags. The gunpowder was manufactured locally at Camilty explosive works, situated for safety in open countryside on the site of a former mill to the south of West Calder. The works ceased production at the end of the 1920s and were demolished in September 1931. Today the co-op's centrally-managed modern equivalent, Scotmid, still trades in Main Street. The role which the movement played in the lives of West Calder families is recalled by the buildings in Society Lane and Society Place which all formed part of its local shopping empire. Amongst the premises were a bakery, stables and coach houses, the latter of which were later converted into garages for the co-op's fleet of mobile shops and delivery vans. Part of the society's former premises is now used by the West Calder Workspace initiative.

West Calder's earliest school was situated near the Auld Kirk and later moved to the appropriately named School Lane, which formerly branched off Main Street. A primary school was subsequently built in Stewart Street. The buildings seen here made up the premises of West Calder High, but pupils who wished to go on to further education had to travel each day by train to Boroughmuir High School in Edinburgh. In 1921, however, West Calder became a fully fledged post-intermediate senior secondary school, meaning that local pupils took their leaving certificate examinations there. The first higher passes were achieved the following March, while Mr Jack was headmaster. To equip the buildings for their new role, the gym was extended in 1923 and a new wing of classrooms was added during the 1930s. During the Second World War over 500 of the school's former pupils served in the armed forces. In 1949, when peace was restored and the post-war Labour government raised the school leaving age from fourteen to fifteen years, HORSA huts ('Hut Operation for the Raising of the School [leaving] Age') had to be erected in the grounds to cope with the increase in pupil numbers. West Calder High transferred to a new site at Polbeth in 1965 and primary education is now provided elsewhere too: at Parkhead School, on a site at the east end of the town, and at St Mary's RC, Polbeth, near the new high school. Of the buildings shown here, that on the right has been demolished, the one in the middle has been converted into houses, and the janitor's bungalow is also now a private house. Glimpsed behind the telegraph pole is the classroom which housed the art department where Mr Ario Santini, himself a former pupil, inspired many boys and girls to enjoy his subject. It too is now a house, behind which a modern leisure centre has been built.

'Knees bend, arms stretch' may well have been the teacher's command as these boys in serried rows underwent a session of PT in the front playground of West Calder High School. PT stood officially for physical training, but in the days long before child-centred education had been thought of this was often translated by the boys as 'physical torture', partly because PE teachers, or 'drillies' as they were often known, were famed for their strict discipline including stinging strokes of the strap for those who forgot their gym kit or dared to slack during lessons. Among other changes, the growth in the school roll following the Second World War resulted in the existing two school houses known as Picts and Scots being augmented by a third, Gaels, competing both in the realms of classroom scholarship and sport for the coveted prize quaich, which was awarded at the end of each academic year. While pupils were divided within the school into three competing houses, all were proud to wear the school's badge depicting a lion rampant, and never more so than when in the summer of 1953 – although the smallest school competing – West Calder High won the Mid Lothian County School Sports. By this time Mr Ligertwood had been rector for three years, having succeeded the long-serving Mr Brydone in 1950 (he had occupied the post since 1926). Mr Ligertwood supervised the move when the school transferred to its new site at Polbeth in 1965. Boys and girls at West Calder High continued to be segregated for PE until after the move, when mixed sessions in the gym and on the playing fields were gradually introduced.

The spire of the United Free Church rises in the background of this view of Main Street looking east. Beyond the newsagent's on the left is the facade of Thomson's Pie Shop (see page 19), and rising above it the bottom section of the famous Thistle Tower.

16

The Thistle Tower was one of West Calder's best-known landmarks. It was built by local benefactor John Thomson, or Pie Jock as he was affectionately known after the pie shop from which he made his wealth (and which was overlooked by the tower).

East End, West Calder

The Thistle Tower was constructed by local builder Mr Fairley, whose design was inspired by a visit to the World Fair in Chicago. It boasted a clock with three faces, and it was claimed that to ensure the chime of the clock was unique, Pie Jock sent a local fiddler round all the other public clocks in West and Mid Lothian to listen to them strike the hour and make sure the notes chimed by the bells in West Calder were different from any others.

The thistle-topped spire which gave West Calder's best-known landmark its name features prominently on this morale-boosting greetings card, sent to many local men and women serving in the forces. In May 1949 the Thistle Tower was demolished, and a report in the local weekly newspaper mourned its loss, describing its passing into history as 'like the death of an old friend'.

Wearing starched white aprons, the staff of John Thomson's pie shop gather at the door of the premises for a photograph. The mutton pies which they baked could be enjoyed by customers seated at tables in the 'Refreshment Rooms' advertised on the window to the left, but with their crisp, water pastry shells could also be eaten as one of the earliest forms of takeaway food, and were often enjoyed by those hurrying to attend performances at the nearby People's Palace Theatre which the enterprising Mr Thomson also owned. Long-demolished, the People's Palace stood on the Cleugh Brae near the spot now occupied by the premises of the Royal Bank of Scotland.

Keep
smiling

Greetings
-to a' West Cauther bairns,
Wherever ye may be,
At outposts in the hameland,
Or faur ayont the sea,
Frae leal herts in your auld toon,
Who mind ye aye the same,
An' wait the day your eident feet,
Will a' come troopin' hame.

Under the ownership of Pie Jock Thomson, the People's Palace Theatre hosted many famous Scottish variety artists including Sir Harry Lauder. On other occasions it was used for meetings, and in November 1870, during the famous Mid Lothian Campaign, future Prime Minister William Ewart Gladstone spoke from its stage to a crowded audience as part of his successful election campaign. Later Gladstone returned as Prime Minister and spoke again at the People's Palace on 17 November 1885. Prime Ministers Balfour, McDonald and Lord Rosebery all also spoke at the People's Palace. Later in its long and varied career the venue featured roller skating as an attraction and during the 1920s and 30s the lower level became Nannie Mullen's Picture House, a use to which it was easily adapted as its situation on the Cleugh Brae provided a natural slope for the rows of cinema seats. The Brae is now the site of the local Royal Bank of Scotland branch, which in 2003 celebrated the 125th anniversary of its establishment in West Calder.

MAIN St WEST CALDER.   R.BRAID.

This view of Main Street features on a postcard sent in 1908 and looks to the east with the co-op clock in the middle distance on the right. In the era before widespread motorised transport, carts were generally used for door-to-door deliveries, including those made twice-daily by West Calder's five dairies in order to ensure that customers received their milk while it was still fresh. Amongst the dairies was Russell's in Hartwood Road from which the well-known transport and haulage business grew.

The west end of Main Street was busy with pedestrians but devoid of traffic when this postcard was produced in the early 1900s. R. Wells Brown's chemist's shop can be seen on the right, marked by the mortar and pestle sign.

St Mary's Chapel (left) at the West End of West Calder still stands, but is now dedicated to Our Lady and St Bridget. The town's Catholic population grew significantly as a result of the late nineteenth century shale oil boom and the attendant influx of workers from Ireland. The two-storey block on the right now houses the West End Hotel. In the middle distance is the steeple of the West Kirk of Calder.

MAIN St. WEST CALDER.

R. BRAID.

The junction of Main Street with Dickson Street (right). Many of the buildings seen here have now been demolished, and the modern premises of Lindsay & Gilmour's pharmacy stand nearby with flats above. West Calder's former Regal Cinema was situated near here.

Canvas awnings protected the goods in the window of Jocky McCabe's greengrocer's shop (left) when this more modern view of Main Street looking east was taken. The shop on the corner on the right with the hanging baskets outside was the premises of well-known West Calder butcher Mr G. Halliday. As well as his shop on the south side of Main Street, Mr Halliday also served customers in the villages around West Calder from a van. Further east on the south side of Main Street there used to be an ironmonger's, a sweet shop and a tea room, as well as the newsagent's belonging to Catherine Tennant of which Allen Douglas's paper shop is the modern successor. The decorative metal crown on top of the three-storey co-op building, a familiar West Calder landmark, can be glimpsed in the background on the left.

LIMEFIELD ROAD, WEST-CALDER.

Looking west along the length of Limefield Road towards the United Free Church. Prime Minister William Ewart Gladstone, MP for the local constituency of Mid Lothian, once spoke in the church. The appearance of this section of Limefield Road has changed little since this photograph was taken.

Further out of town, the stretch of Limefield Road that linked West and Mid Calder was still a rural tree-lined byway when this postcard was produced in the early years of the twentieth century. It has now developed into a busy main road. It was this route that post runner Alex Kelly followed six days a week when he carried the Royal Mail from Mid Calder to West Calder, a duty he performed for 21 years. He carried a horn which he blew to announce his noontime arrival. West Calder obtained its own post office in May 1839, just before the introduction of the Penny Post in 1840 which resulted in a large increase in deliveries.

ON LIMEFIELD ROAD, WEST CALDER. R.BRAID.

ON LIMEFIELD BRIDGE NEAR BELLSQUARRY, WEST CALDER. PHOTO. R.BRAID.

Limefield Bridge spans the River Almond.

The new place of worship that superseded the Auld Kirk was what is described as the Established Church on this postcard. This fine building with its tall spire still stands on the south side of Main Street at the west end of the town. Belonging to the Church of Scotland, it is now the West Kirk of Calder. One of West Calder's ministers, the Revd John Muckersy, is credited with founding an early savings bank. It operated during the 1840s and to join it members had to invest a minimum of half a crown. Each quarter a penny's interest was paid on every five shillings deposited in each account. West Calder also had its own friendly society which was founded in 1809 and provided benefits for its subscribers in times of need.

The Victorian villa on the left was the manse for the minister of the United Presbyterian Church at Harwood on the outskirts of West Calder. Its congregation was formed in 1794 and for nearly a century worshipped in what was known as the Meeting House until the church seen here was built in 1874. In 1962 it moved to the neighbouring village of Polbeth, where the church is called Polbeth Harwood Parish Church, thus acknowledging its origins. This bright attractive place of worship welcomes visitors as part of the Churches to Visit in Scotland scheme. The old manse seen in this view still stands but is now a private house. The church has been demolished, only a single stone cross from it surviving to be preserved in the peaceful inner courtyard of the new premises in Polbeth, which were completed in 1972.

OPENING WEST-CALDER BOWLING & TENNIS SEASON 1908.

The official opening of West Calder Bowling and Tennis Club at the start of the 1908 season. The club's green is situated at the east end of the town, to the south of Limefield UF Church, which is in the background of this view. The quaint wooden Victorian pavilion seen here has long since been replaced by a more substantial brick clubhouse to the west of the green. Lawn bowls is still a popular pastime in West Calder, but as the club's name suggests it also once boasted tennis courts, which were well-used by many of its younger members. During the 1920s and 30s tournaments and inter-club matches were played, and there was sufficient interest in the sport for two additional courts to be opened in West Calder in 1928.

BOWLING GREEN, WEST CALDER

The groundsman at West Calder Bowling and Tennis Club cuts the green before a match. While bowls and tennis were popular, the biggest sporting occasion of the year in West Calder was the fair and athletics meeting held at Burngrange Park on the final Friday in July. Later the event was moved to the last Saturday in the month and professional athletes took part in the races for cash prizes, although one popular race was always restricted to local miners. Another much-anticipated annual event was the cattle show, which was held in a field at Limefield. As well as the judging and parading of livestock, this also featured classes for horses and ponies. For several years local girl Jenny Thornton was a favourite with the crowd in the show-jumping event.

Gillon's family grocers stood on the corner of Union Street, which branched off Main Street on its south side. Neighbouring shops included Wilson's fish shop and Dick Mullen's fruit shop, beyond which was the Vennel. The name Vennel derived from the French verb *venir* meaning to come, in the same way as the word alley comes from the French *aller* meaning to go. In West Calder the Vennel was the site of the town's Model Lodging House, which provided economical accommodation for itinerant workers and local people who were destitute. Residents shared dormitories and a 'model' set of rules governed the running of the establishment. These ranged from a ban on the consumption of alcohol to the times each day that residents were allowed to occupy the dormitories. Now only one building in what was formerly Union Street remains standing: the house which was the home of West Calder's well-known scrap metal dealers, the Flannigan family, who still live in the town. The spire of the United Presbyterian Church at Harburn is seen in the background to the south.

Registered SY 660, this solid-tyred Edwardian charabanc was built by the Belsize company in Manchester. The postcard was published by James Philip of West Calder and is thought to show a group of local people on a day out. Even on this social occasion it was de rigueur for both men and women to wear hats. In the unfortunate event of rain spoiling the day a canvas canopy could be unfolded from the rear to provide the passengers with some protection, although the sides of the vehicle remained open to the elements.

The long, low lines of miners' rows which were hurriedly built to provide rented homes for West Calder's shale miners and their large families were given distinctive nicknames to mark them out from their drearily similar neighbours. This postcard bears the hand-written caption 'The Happy Land', which was the local name for the 302 houses in this crowded development. It shows many of the row's inhabitants, both young and old, posing for the visiting photographer. The person who sent it added the note: 'Do not mistake this for "Paradise" ', which was the local name for a neighbouring street of similar rows. The Parish of West Calder's population rose dramatically from 2,120 in 1851 to 7,900 in 1884 as a result of the oil boom.

This battlemented folly stands in the grounds of Auchenhard Farm (spelt on the postcard as 'Auchinhard') at Westwood between West Calder and Addiewell. It is known as Ivy Tower, and does appropriately have ivy entwining its way around its walls.

Westwood House, with its imposing central tower and ivy-clad walls, no longer graces the West Calder landscape as it lies buried below the tons of pink shale waste which make up the huge Five Sisters bings. The attractive mansion, which was a well-known landmark on the road between West Calder and Addiewell, was built by a wealthy Edinburgh lawyer called Smith in the days when this part of the County of Mid Lothian was a delightful rural retreat where the professional classes could enjoy peaceful weekends away from their busy city jobs, and yet be within comparatively easy reach of work when Monday morning came round. Westwood was later bought by a Mr Baird, but he appears to have run into financial difficulties and soon afterwards sold the property to a Mr Steuart, whose son Captain Robert Steuart was the occupant at the time this postcard view was produced in the early years of the twentieth century. His obituary in the *West Lothian Courier* (14 March 1913) said of Westwood: 'Although the land, agriculturally, is not of a rich, fertile nature, the estate is a valuable one from the minerals point of view. Part of the shale minerals on the estate have already been worked by the Addiewell Oil Company . . . The 'Dunnit' shale seam, which is supposed to be the best of the lot, has not yet been wrought on the estate, but we understand that the Oakbank Company will shortly begin operations with this end in view.' The fact that this substantial mansion could be sacrificed to the advancing shale bing gives an impression of both how much waste material was produced by the mineral oil industry, and how lucrative shale extraction was.

BELLSQUARRY.   R.BRAID. PHOTO.

Local photographer Robert Braid of Livingston Village took this picture of a pipe band leading a parade past the Elm Tree Inn in the village of Bellsquarry. The banner reads 'Bellsquarry Picnic', but it is not clear what the event is celebrating. The horse-drawn vehicles seen outside the inn may well have belonged to Barclay & Sons carriage hirers, whose premises behind the inn are advertised on the gable wall. The Elm Tree saw a variety of uses over the years but is now vacant and in a dilapidated state, whereas Bellsquarry has grown into a desirable residential suburb on the southern outskirts of Livingston New Town. Hopefully with an increase in the number of residents, and with Bellsquarry School recently extended to full primary status, growing local prosperity will encourage a new owner to purchase the old Elm Tree and safeguard its future.

The Elm Tree Inn is glimpsed again here beyond the row of houses called School Terrace situated in Calders Road, Bellsquarry. The cottage just visible nearest the camera on the left has changed little in the century since this photograph was taken, but first floor dormers have been added to its neighbours opposite.

Newly built Mid Lothian County Council houses face older cottage properties on the opposite side of Bellsquarry's broad Main Street in this 1930s view of the village. Beyond the two blocks of new houses, which each contained four homes, Bellsquarry Primary School can be glimpsed. Threatened at one time with closure because of its falling roll, so many new families have chosen attractive Bellsquarry for their home that the old school has now had to be extended with the building of additional classrooms to cope with growing pupil numbers.

Situated to the south of West Calder, Cobbinshaw was also served by rail and there were hopes in Victorian times that this hamlet would grow into a flourishing spa resort. The station which served it was sited 100 yards from a large reservoir which its owners, the Caledonian Railway, kept well-stocked with brown trout. The enterprising railway company sold fishing rights to anglers at Cobbinshaw and also promoted the pleasant walks around the shores of the reservoir, which covers 500 acres and whose banks are seven miles in circumference. This extensive man-made body of water predated the coming of the railway. The area was surveyed in 1820 and after the completion of a retaining dam in 1822 was flooded to provide a supply of water for the Union Canal, which also opened to navigation in the same year. Although a proposed health resort – which could perhaps have become as large and famous as the railway-owned Gleneagles Hotel and golf club established in Perthshire in the 1920s – was never constructed, Cobbinshaw remained popular with fishermen and curlers into the twentieth century.

Cobbinshaw Station and Loch

In contrast with its attractions as a place of recreation and sport, Cobbinshaw was also an industrial centre. In 1870 the South Cobbinshaw Oil Company built houses on the reservoir's southern shore to serve its nearby mine and oil works. At the 1891 census, 97 people were recorded as occupying nineteen houses (many only comprising a single room). There was also a company school and other industrial features included a brickworks, with a limestone mine superseding the shale mine when the oil works closed in 1875. By 1891 there were 52 houses and 265 residents, with industrial activity continuing into the twentieth century under a number of different owners. When the Caledonian Mineral Oil Co. went out of business in 1903 the houses were emptied, but the local minister rented thirteen of them for a number of years, remaining in the area until 1938, by which date the dwindling village had essentially vanished. (Information extracted from *Shale Oil Scotland* by David Kerr, 1999.)

Cobbinshaw Farm is seen in the foreground with the railway station beyond in this rural view. In winter the reservoir's frozen surface was popular with curlers, and when the ice was deemed thick enough huge crowds ventured out on to it to watch the bonspiels which were played there. As the granite curling stones trundled across the ice they created a rumbling noise, and it was this rather than the cheers of the spectators which led to the sport being nicknamed the 'roaring game'. Water from the reservoir was channelled into the Union Canal via a series of tunnels and aqueducts which followed the Almond Valley through Almondell Estate and Calderwood Country Park. Demand for supplies was so great that the reservoir had to be extended between 1842 and 1849, after which it became the largest inland body of water in Mid Lothian.

An Addiewell oil works shunting engine is seen pulling a row of wagons laden with shale towards the makeshift level crossing in front of Graham Street in this postcard view. The street, seen on the left with its long low lines of brick-built miners' rows, was named after Professor Thomas Graham, the Scot on the staff of University College London who invited James 'Paraffin' Young to come south, and did much to advance his career, a fact which the oil pioneer never forgot and for which he was always grateful.

Addiewell is served by a station on the former Caledonian line between Edinburgh Princes Street and Glasgow Central Stations. The station opened on 9 July 1869.

Originally the home of oil pioneer James 'Paraffin' Young and his family while he supervised work on his new Addiewell oil works in 1864, this villa is described in the postcard caption as Addiewell Parish Church Manse. It was indeed home to the parish minister from the 1870s until 1929. That year, however, the long-standing rift between the Church of Scotland and the Free Church of Scotland was healed in Addiewell (as in many Scottish towns and villages) and as the two congregations reunited, homes for two ministers were no longer required. Surplus, therefore, to the church's requirements, the manse which had been rented from Paraffin Young's oil company was let to a local farmer. It was later purchased by his tenants, well-known local farming family the Barries, and continues to serve as the farmhouse for Auchenhard Farm to the present day.

Three of the village of Addiewell's landmark buildings are seen in this postcard view: the primary school (on the left), the co-operative society store and the tollhouse where the horse-drawn carriage is seen stopping to pay to use this stretch of road. Educationally, Addiewell is known today for its combined St Thomas RC and Addiewell Primary Schools, in which denominational and non-denominational pupils share not only the same playground but the same building.

Many of West Calder's miners worked at Westwood Mine which was situated to the north of the town towards Addiewell. Some of the hutches which were used to carry the shale from the mine to the oil refineries are seen lined up in the foreground. It was at Burngrange, West Calder's other mine, that the Scottish shale oil industry's worst ever disaster occurred on 10 January 1947, towards the end of the afternoon shift, which was being worked by a total of 76 miners. Two explosions rocked the mine at 8 p.m., and the blasts blew the three men nearest to the source off their feet, knocking one of them unconscious. His two companions helped carry him by stretcher to the surface, but he died before they could seek medical help. Burngrange had such a safe reputation that the manager refused to believe the explosions had occurred, although he summoned a doctor to attend to the fatally-injured man.

Instead of calling the mines rescue team, the manager insisted on going underground himself to assess the damage, accompanied by the overman. Once below ground they soon realised the extent of the tragedy as it became apparent that the two blasts had started a fire raging. Fourteen other miners were cut off behind the flames. Back at the surface both the mines rescue team and the local fire brigade were summoned, and they tackled the blaze for the next four days. It was not until 14 January that they succeeded in reaching the trapped miners, all of whom had been suffocated by carbon monoxide gas. The fifteen men who died were: Henry Cowie, David Carroll, William Carroll, George Easton, John Fairley, William Findlay, Anthony Gaughan, William Greenock, Thomas Heggie, John Lightbody, John McGarty, James McCauley, David Muir, Samuel Pake and William Ritchie. This picture shows three of the famous Five Sisters bings at Westwood oil works. The bings have been 'A'-listed and it has been suggested that they could be utilised as a tourist attraction, with a cable car to carry visitors to one of their lofty summits and dry ski runs developed on their slopes.

Main Street, Stoneyburn, showing the Miners' Institute and some of the miners' rows. Local colliery-owners the Loganlea Coal Company built the first houses in 1897 and by the end of the year 87 of these modest homes had been erected, along with a shop and a pub. Only 22 families had moved in by this date, but expansion was rapid and by 1899 there were 98 families living in Stoneyburn, with 48 more houses under construction. The institute (left) was built in 1901 and provided miners not only with indoor sports facilities, including billiards and darts, but also a small library and a reading room which was supplied with daily newspapers. The village's first public primary school was opened in 1902 and after a long campaign a separate Roman Catholic primary was opened in 1941. The new denominational primary became known for its long-serving head teachers, with the first head, John McKeon, in charge until 1957 when he was succeeded by Pat Mahon who remained in the post until 1967. He in turn was followed by Jimmy McCue, Mrs R. Alison, Mrs Scanlon, and finally in 1985 by Mrs Mary Murphy.

Hermand House dates from 1797 and is located south of Polbeth. It was damaged by fire in 1970 but has since been restored and converted into flats. The estate was known as Herdmanshiells when it was purchased by well-known Edinburgh lawyer George Fergusson (who had been called to the bar in 1765), and it was he who commissioned the building of the mansion seen here. Its main architectural feature is the front door with its substantial pediment, approached by a short flight of stairs. In 1799 Fergusson was made a Scottish law lord and adopted a variation of the name of his estate for his title, Lord Hermand. As his wife was the niece of Lord Cockburn, Hermand often features in the latter's writings in which family loyalty fails to conceal that he was a heavy drinker, also revealing that his love of the bottle often softened his judgements on those who appeared before him as a result of imbibing too liberally. As his duties as a law lord only occupied six months of the year,

Hermand had ample time to devote to his West Calder estate, where he carried out many improvements including spreading lime on his fields to reduce moss. He waged a war on weeds and designed a special instrument consisting of a bamboo cane with a billhook attached to the end of it, with which he scythed them down, even when making his way to church on Sundays. He once became so engrossed in this task that he arrived after the service was over. On his outings to church he was accompanied by his large, black Newfoundland dog, Dolphin, who joined him in the family pew where he amused the rest of the congregation by resting his paws on the hymn book shelf in a prayer-like position. Even on those Sundays when his lordship failed to attend church, Dolphin is said to have arrived and sat through the whole of the service before trotting home to Hermand House. Many stories are told about Lord Hermand's convivial parties at the big house, but despite his drinking – which he declared was one of his virtues – he lived to the age of 84, dying in 1827.

LIMEFIELD HOUSE WEST-CALDER.

While in residence at Limefield House (built in 1806) near Polbeth, James 'Paraffin' Young welcomed his friend from student days, Dr David Livingstone, when he was on furlough from his missionary explorations in Africa. During one of his holidays Dr Livingstone entertained the children of the family by constructing an imitation African kraal of small huts in the garden. The celebrated explorer also planted a tree at Limefield to commemorate his stay. In 1954 the mansion was gifted for conversion into a home for the elderly, but this was closed in the late 1990s as it was not possible to bring the attractive Georgian mansion up to the standard of accommodation then required for caring for older residents.